The CBT Art Activity Book

of related interest

The Big Book of Therapeutic Activity Ideas for Children and Teens
Inspiring Arts-Based Activities and Character Education Curricula
Lindsey Joiner
ISBN 978 1 84905 865 0
eISBN 978 0 85700 447 5

Mandala Symbolism and Techniques
Innovative Approaches for Professionals
Susan I. Buchalter
ISBN 978 1 84905 889 6
eISBN 978 0 85700 593 9

Creative Expression Activities for Teens
Exploring Identity through Art, Craft and Journaling
Bonnie Thomas
ISBN 978 1 84905 842 1
eISBN 978 0 85700 417 8

Raising Self-Esteem in Adults
An Eclectic Approach with Art Therapy, CBT and DBT Based Techniques
Susan I. Buchalter
ISBN 978 1 84905 966 4
eISBN 978 0 85700 821 3

Helping Adolescents and Adults to Build Self-Esteem
A Photocopiable Resource Book
Deborah M. Plummer
ISBN 978 1 84905 425 6
eISBN 978 0 85700 794 0

Teen Anxiety
A CBT and ACT Activity Resource Book for Helping Anxious Adolescents
Raychelle Cassada Lohmann
ISBN 978 1 84905 969 5
eISBN 978 0 85700 859 6

The CBT Art Activity Book

100 illustrated handouts for creative therapeutic work

Jennifer Guest

Jessica Kingsley *Publishers*
London and Philadelphia

First published in 2016
by Jessica Kingsley Publishers
73 Collier Street
London N1 9BE, UK
and
400 Market Street, Suite 400
Philadelphia, PA 19106, USA

www.jkp.com

Library of Congress Cataloging in Publication Data
Guest, Jennifer.
The CBT art activity book : 100 illustrated handouts for creative therapeutic work / Jennifer Guest.
pages cm
Includes bibliographical references.
ISBN 978-1-84905-665-6 (alk. paper)
1. Cognitive therapy–Handbooks, manuals, etc. I. Title.
RC489.C63G83 2016
616.89'1425–dc23
2015016682

British Library Cataloguing in Publication Data
A CIP catalogue record for this book is available from the British Library

ISBN 978 1 84905 665 6
eISBN 978 1 78450 168 6

Printed and bound in Great Britain

For Oscar and Jessamy, both forever inspirational and amazing.

Acknowledgements

I would like to express my thanks and gratitude to all the clients and colleagues I've had the pleasure of working with over the years, people who have knowingly, or not, helped bring these designs into being. The worksheets have been developed in response to many hard-working and enthusiastic clients, in combination with the ideas gratefully received from Cognitive Behavioural Therapy and art therapy pioneers. I would also like to thank everyone from Jessica Kingsley Publishers who has had a part in making this book available to so many more people.

Contents

About This Book

The worksheets in the first part of this book are intended for use within therapeutic situations by qualified professionals. They have been developed from the premises of Cognitive Behavioural Therapy techniques, to be used as creative tools in aiding therapeutic work with adults and young people, individuals and groups. As any therapist will know, an emotionally safe space is paramount when encouraging others to explore their deepest feelings. Emotional disclosure can be challenging for clients and leave them feeling incredibly vulnerable. Respect and compassion for this, as for any artwork and written work produced by clients, is an essential part of therapy as well.

The worksheets can be used at various points throughout therapy, either individually or as packs made up with the relevant pages, to complement the theme of the therapy. The pages can help in identifying areas of focus, with themes such as anger management, building self-esteem or clarifying goals. The chapters in Part One are grouped into three broad areas of focus: developing a sense of self and building confidence; managing emotions; problem solving and identifying goals. Part Two comprises of two chapters, the first is made up of letters of the alphabet, the second a collection of mandalas. They are not ordered in this way with the intention of working through the book from beginning to end, but rather to be used with the therapist's discretion as to the most appropriate and helpful pages for each client. It is assumed that professionals using this section of the book would be doing so with prior knowledge of their client's presenting issues and mental health levels, using this knowledge to make ethical and sensitive choices.

The chapters are laid out for ease of access, so that the most relevant pages can be found easily. There is overlap between many of them, meaning that some worksheets are included in two or in all of the chapters. There is also some duplication in the focus of the worksheets, as one particular worksheet may appeal more to one client or age group than another. It is certainly not an exhaustive or definitive collection.

Introduction

There are many Cognitive Behavioural Therapy (CBT) worksheets and visual resources available for therapeutic work. An example is the impressive resource book *Helping Adolescents and Adults to Build Self-Esteem* by Deborah Plummer (2005). I thought it would be useful in my clinical practice to develop this idea of having visual stimuli by combining the techniques used in CBT with some aspects of art as therapy. *The CBT Art Activity Book* is a collection of the worksheets I designed with CBT, art therapy and aesthetics in mind. It was a revelation to discover that the hand-drawn images and patterns were a refreshing sight for people living in a world saturated with computer generated, 'perfect' images.

Many of my clients have been inspired to draw after working with these worksheets. The fact that they are drawn by hand seems to allow people to be creative with more confidence, freeing them to make visual mistakes whilst enjoying the therapeutic benefits of working creatively. Inviting clients to create their own artwork can be less daunting for them after being reminded that it's okay to have a resulting piece of work that does not look like it was produced by a computer. It's the process of creating that generates the therapeutic value, not how a piece of artwork looks at the end of the process. Being creative can be extremely cathartic.

I've derived a great deal of pleasure in drawing and designing these pages. It can feel meditative and mindful to be lost in doing something we truly love, giving our minds time to be free from thinking or worrying. I came to this way of drawing through many years of passionate doodling. For anyone interested in learning how to draw in this style, it has been named 'Zentangle' by artists Maria Thomas and Rick Roberts (2012). They have released some fantastic practical books and online resources, teaching how to produce similar artwork.

This book provides an opportunity for people to be inspired by the worksheets and to help people communicate visually, with or without words. It is hoped that there will be an array of art materials available for clients to use with this book, and that the pages may act as prompts for further artwork to be created on a much larger scale.

The first part contains worksheets for therapeutic purposes. The second part contains illustrated letters of the alphabet for colouring in and potentially cutting out, which can be used as an extension of 'sense of self' work. In this section there is also a collection of mandala designs to be coloured in for pure enjoyment.

Part One – Worksheets Collection

Cognitive Behavioural Therapy Concepts

The idea for these worksheets came about from using CBT techniques within my own clinical practice. Although it is expected that the worksheets in Part One will be used primarily by therapists familiar with these techniques, here is a very brief outline of this major form of psychotherapy.

CBT helps clients to understand how thoughts and patterns of thinking affect their feelings and behaviour, including physiological aspects. The concepts were developed by Aaron Beck, an American psychiatrist working at the University of Pennsylvania in the early 1960s. Originally CBT was intended for researching and treating depression (Beck 1995). Since then, CBT has broadened into applications for treating a wide range of mental health and emotional wellbeing issues and is used extensively as an evidence-based psychotherapy (Neenan and Drydan 2004).

There is a widespread belief amongst many people that it is external events or other people which are to blame for how they are feeling, especially when these feelings are anger, upset, disappointment, distress or anxiety. CBT aims to challenge and dispel this idea by helping clients understand that there are a variety of perceptions we can have about how we view the world and our experiences. If this were not the case, then all our feelings and reactions would be identical to one another's. It is evident that it is our interpretation of an event which determines how we feel about it. It is therefore essential that to make a change in the way we feel about external events and experiences, we need to make changes in the way we think about them. Our interpretations are wholly subjective and open to being distorted, and can be inaccurate. People often mistake their interpretations for facts, without realising the difference between the two.

Emotional wellbeing can be severely affected when the assimilations of our experiences begin to exist as negative beliefs, particularly when these are in relation to ourselves, our competencies and ultimately our self-worth. CBT aims to enable people to acknowledge this, so that a different perception can be chosen, which will affect how that person feels. This may serve to negate or minimise the problem. This is not to say that we consciously create emotional problems by our negative thinking and beliefs, but that when external events happen in our lives our perceptions can help or hinder how we manage and deal with the effects of the event (Neenan and Drydan 2004).

Psychologist Albert Ellis (1997) developed the 'ABC model' to demonstrate how our thoughts affect our feelings, which in turn affect our behaviour:

Activating event...................................leads to

Beliefs – based on interpretations...................................leads to

Consequences – emotional and behavioural.

This model illustrates the concept of changing our thoughts and ways of thinking first, in order to alter the ways we feel and make changes in our behaviour. The beliefs are defined as three different levels of cognition:

1. Core beliefs

These kinds of thoughts are statements we make to ourselves, which have often become fixed, inaccurate and damaging to our self-esteem. They are often referred to as schemas, and are believed to be the deepest level of thought. Core beliefs inform how we interpret our experiences because we focus on selecting information from events that confirm these, and filter out information that contradicts them.

High emotion can be an indicator that there are fundamental core beliefs underpinning what is initially being expressed. Helping clients become aware of these can be hugely enlightening and empowering for therapeutic change. Once recognised, clients can then aim to return to a more logical, evidence-based way of processing information (Beck 1995).

2. Intermediate beliefs

These usually lie in between our core beliefs and automatic thoughts. They are often defined as being rules, attitudes and assumptions, and are affected by our core beliefs. Usually we are only semi-aware of our intermediate beliefs, and so they are often unarticulated (Beck 1995).

3. Automatic thoughts

These thoughts are the ones that continually run through our mind, and can be verbal or visual. They make up the inner, running commentary often described as 'self-talk'. They are usually situation-specific and considered the most superficial of the three levels of thinking. Some theorists define these as 'negative automatic thoughts' (NATs). If we are experiencing distress, these have a detrimental impact on our thinking. A correlation can be made between our level of emotional upset and how logically we are thinking. Once again, these automatic thoughts can become habitual patterns we might not be fully aware of until we do some exploration after the distressing event or situation (Neenan and Drydan 2004).

The three interactive levels of how we think can each be a focus within therapy. It is common for CBT to begin at the NATs level, facilitating clients to become aware of the nature of their inner self-talk, before shifting the focus towards them becoming aware of their underlying assumptions and rules, and their core beliefs (Neenan and Drydan 2004).

The habitual nature of our thoughts and belief systems can lead us to feel safe in their familiarity, even when they no longer serve us. Despite recognising this, there can be a resistance to change because it falls into the realms of the unknown and unfamiliar. To explore and practise new ways of thinking and being can feel scary, so therapy can be a valuable arena.

This book can be considered a vital part of a therapist's toolkit, to be dipped into as and when appropriate, to facilitate the myriad CBT techniques available to challenge and change these non-helpful patterns of thinking. The aesthetic aspect of the worksheets may trigger new revelations for people in recognising the connections and being able to establish more valuable constructs. Rather than forms and columns, the creative nature of the designs may inspire anyone who is searching for a different perspective to problems or feels stuck in their ways of thinking. The worksheets are suited to clients whose communication will be supported by pictures, patterns and images, together with suggestive comments, phrases and questions. Many people's learning is aided and accelerated by doing, and using these worksheets can be an effective way to enhance the experiential aspect of therapy.

Art as Therapy

The process of producing artwork can be incredibly cathartic, informative and affirming for clients in their journey towards change. Communicating through visual means is powerful and can be enlightening, as we often don't have the words to describe or articulate how we are feeling. This can be particularly pertinent where stress and trauma have been experienced. In order to come to terms with such experiences, expressing feelings and memories can be essential for healing.

Art therapist Cathy A. Malchiodi describes how powerful her experiences working within the field of art therapy have been:

> I have been repeatedly taught about important connections between the creative process of image making and health. These experiences have proven to me that art is a potent and effective means of self-expression available to people of all ages and capabilities, that everyone can benefit from art's ability to repair and restore, and that art making as therapy can play a vital role in health, healing, and wholeness... The sensory qualitites of art-making often provide a way for us to tap into our emotions and perceptions more easily than we would with words alone. In cases of emotional trauma, loss, or abuse, art making offers a way to reintegrate complex emotions that are expressed through the senses. Because the tactile aspects of art materials...can be self-soothing and relaxing, art making also may assist the process of emotional reparation and healing...the sensory qualitites of art expression are helpful not only in reducing stress but also in recalling and reframing the felt sense of traumatic memories, grief and loss. (2007, p.xi and p.14)

The psychotherapist Carl Jung was extremely interested in image-work, and he believed that by translating problems and emotions into artwork new and deeper understandings are born. Within his clinical work he used images of his clients' memories and dreams and explored how these connected with their feelings to help them move towards emotional wellbeing and a more robust mental health (Malchiodi 2007).

To create from within ourselves is the paramount goal, with the emphasis being on the process of doing, rather than the aesthetics of the produced artwork. Therefore, no artistic talent is necessary. Supporting clients to express themselves in this way can help them find meaning in how they experience the process. The creative process of making art can bring forth enlightenments and realisations, helping people to cope with conflict resolution, and to process traumatic experiences and overwhelming emotions.

Betty Edwards is the author of the hugely successful book *The New Drawing on the Right Side of the Brain*. She describes her work as a practical demonstration of Roger Sperry's ideas about the duality of our thinking: the left hand side of our brain is where the verbal, analytical thinking happens, the right hand side is where visual and perceptual thinking occurs. Our language system can get in the way of us realising certain information, because its very function is to censor and filter. Edwards believes that insights are made because our language becomes redundant whilst drawing. She goes on to explain how making certain line drawings and doodles can be cathartic because it involves the process of expression:

> 'Analog' drawings are purely expressive drawings, with no nameable objects depicted, using only the expressive quality of line or lines. Unexpectedly, persons untrained in art are able to use this language – that is, produce expressive drawings – and are also able to read the drawings for meaning. (Edwards 2008, p.xiv)

The worksheets and images in Part One are designed to help clients to create their own images, with varying degrees of prompts about focus or content. They can be used as they are or as an inspirational springboard for larger works of art.

Chapter 1

Sense of Self, Self-Esteem Building

Our conscious awareness lets us know that our inner world is made up of thoughts, feelings and reflections. A main part of this awareness is our 'sense of self', our unique identity in relation to the external world. As described by Richard Stevens:

> In part, this is a process of 'I', arising from our sense of engagement and acting within and upon the world, and from our privileged access to the world of inner thoughts and feelings. In part, also, it derives from an awareness of 'me': an image of the kind of person I am. (1996, pp.19–20)

It is fundamental for our mental health and emotional wellbeing to know what we like, what makes us happy, how we feel excited or stimulated and what our fears are. Some worksheets in this chapter are designed to focus on increasing this awareness, bringing our core beliefs about ourselves to the forefront of our consciousness. This can help identify any aspects of our character we would like to develop or diminish.

Self-esteem

Our levels of self-esteem indicate how much we like ourselves, or how high our self-worth is. Self-beliefs have a direct impact on self-esteem levels. It's useful to explore and understand whether our self-beliefs lean towards the positive or negative, identifying the extent to which they help or hinder us in our journey towards emotional wellbeing. Someone with very low levels of self-esteem may struggle to find aspects of themselves that they like or are proud of.

Self-esteem can be raised and damaged by those around us, depending on whether these influences are critical or nourishing. Severe critical parenting, neglect of our childhood needs, a focus on mistakes or overly high expectations can induce low levels of self-esteem, as can major life changes during our adulthood. It is far easier to cope with adverse life events if our self-esteem is at a healthy level beforehand.

We can also feel a range of levels in relation to different areas of our lives. It's important to be aware of these aspects when working with clients, so that the therapy takes into account what feedback a person is receiving from the people in their lives, and how accurate and helpful the internalised information then becomes as a result. It's also important to consider which of these self-beliefs are specific to certain contexts.

The worksheets in this first chapter aim to identify levels of self-esteem. They encourage clients to explore aspects of themselves, their characters and capabilities in a positive way, and to focus on their strengths and skills, so that they may come to celebrate who they are.

Self Beliefs

I CAN DRAW ON FROM MY SURVIVAL KIT

RESOURCES

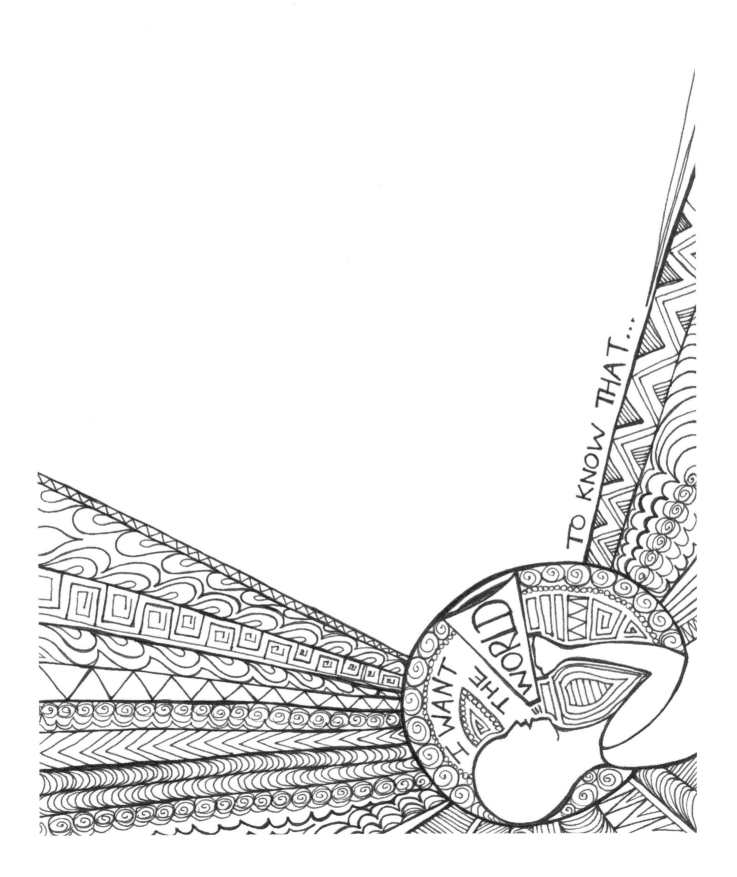

TOP SECRET

THE BEST VIEW

MY FAMILY

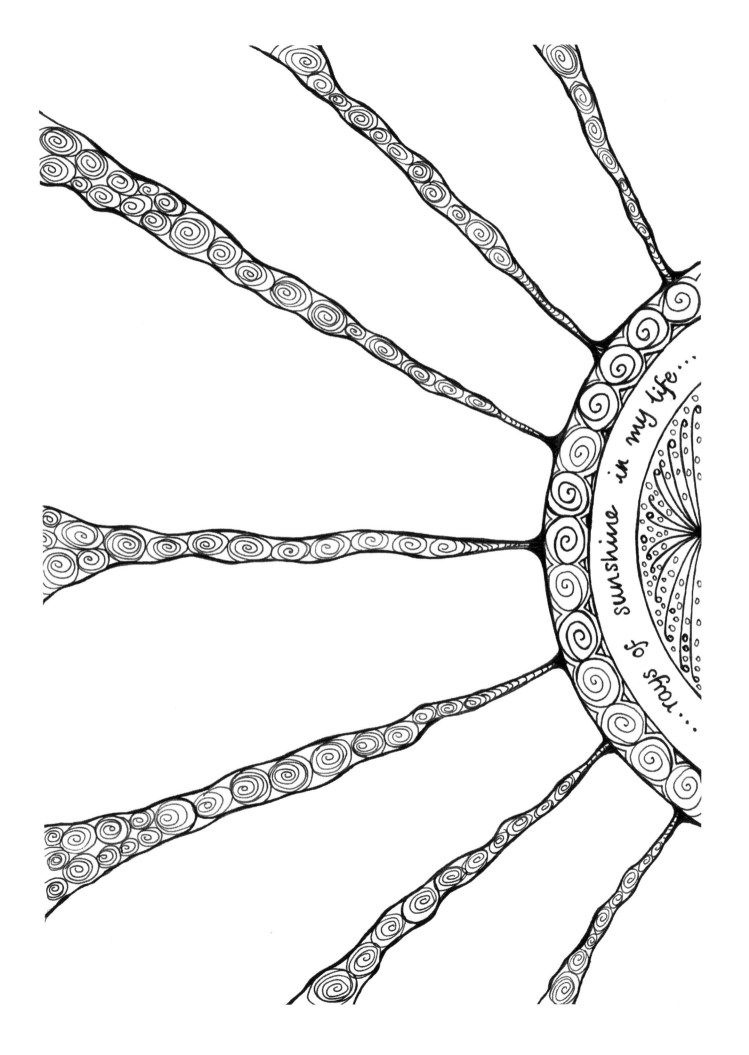

If you were stranded on a desert island who or what would you like with you?

If I was an insect...

the best season weather is...

because...

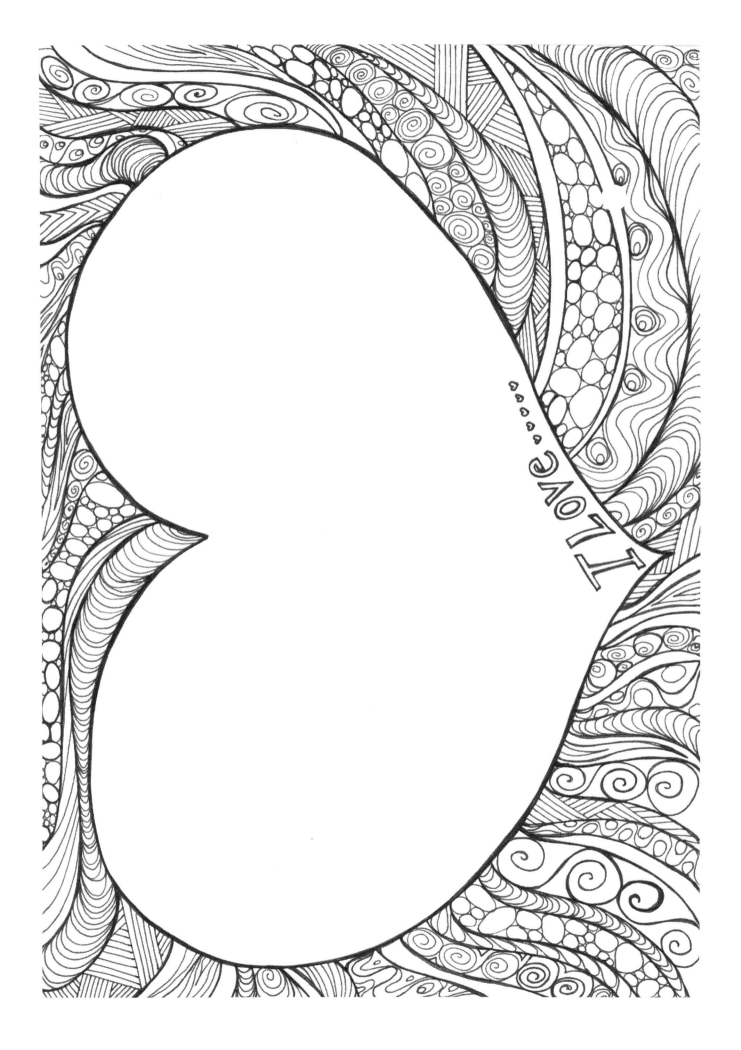

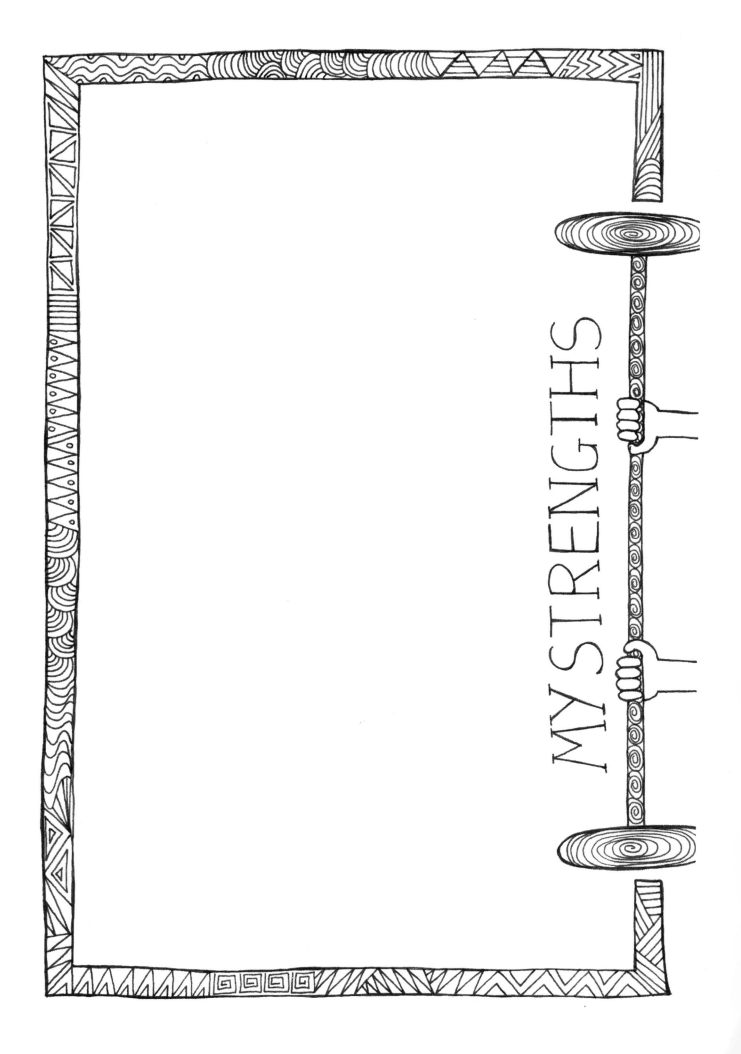

MY STRENGTHS

My favourite meal!

Chapter 2

Managing Emotions, Coping with Loss and Change

Changing our ways of thinking can be productive and helpful for our future wellbeing. Sometimes healing needs to happen first if we have traumas and distressing experiences to come to terms with, or years' worth of repressed emotions. If we have grown up with abuse or neglect, experienced being in an abusive or controlling relationship or suffered a significant loss, there can be a great deal of hurt, pain and anger which can cause problems if continually unexpressed.

Many of us grow up with the idea that it is safe to have and express certain emotions but not others. In adulthood this can often lead to a big build up, and either an explosion or a gradual escaping of the forbidden emotion. Others grow up with the message that their feelings are not important and develop into adults who do not know how they feel because they've been taught not to pay attention to their emotions.

Some clients are often confused and overwhelmed by containing several or conflicting feelings. Processing these through expression can be remedial. It often helps to gain understanding by organising our emotions, especially when we feel in danger of being overwhelmed by them.

If our thoughts are realistic, our emotions are usually a natural response to our experiences. Anxiety is normal to have in situations where we believe there is a threat or that we are in danger, whether the danger is an emotional or physical one. Anger is a natural response to an injustice, to unfair criticism or if we perceive that someone means us harm or does us harm. It is the extent to which anger or anxiety can 'take over' us, and how we express these feelings, that causes problems. Other emotions such as frustration, guilt, hurt and disappointment often masquerade as anger. Grief is a natural response to a loss, which may be the loss of a job, a person or a relationship, and is usually coped with more successfully if there are opportunities for expression.

CBT establishes how realistic our thoughts are in relation to the overwhelming emotion in question, what thoughts heighten the feeling and how our thoughts can help the feeling subside. This can help us to feel empowered and less at the mercy of our emotions. Externalisation techniques can help with this. These separate the feeling out from ourselves, so that it's easier to see that the emotion is not us and we can learn to regain control over our reactions.

The worksheets in this chapter are to help clients reconnect with their emotional world, identify what situations trigger negative thoughts and establish ways that will work for them to feel more in control of their feelings. There are also worksheets at the end of the chapter which focus on processing loss and change.

when I feel confused...

When I feel let down...

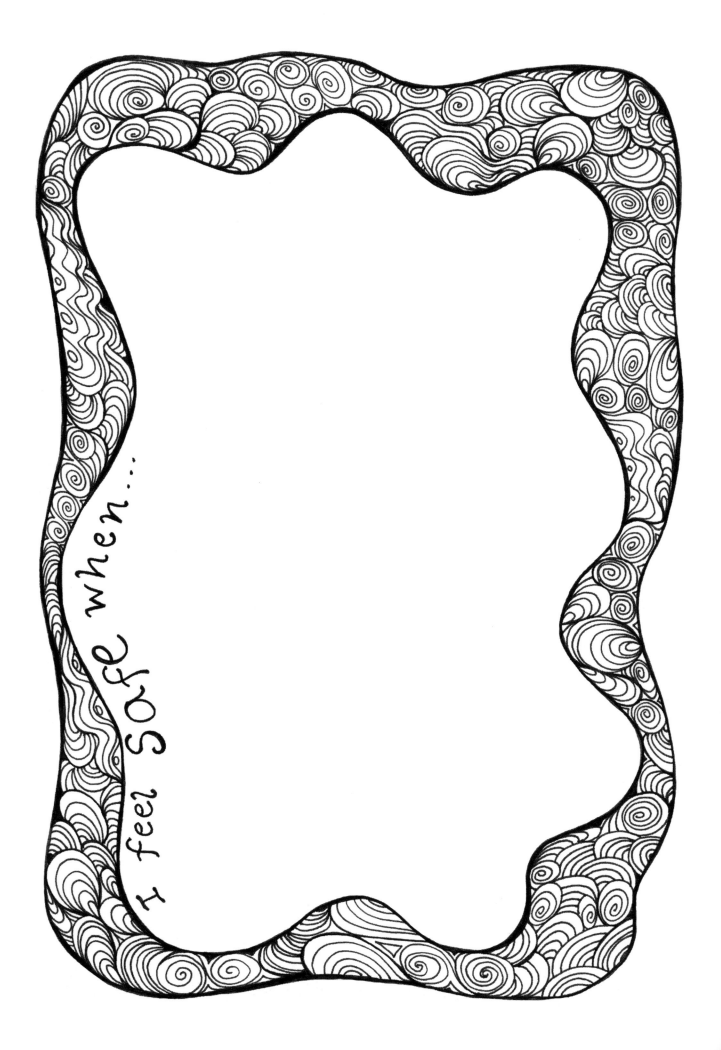

I feel safe when...

when skies are grey...

I feel scared when... ooo

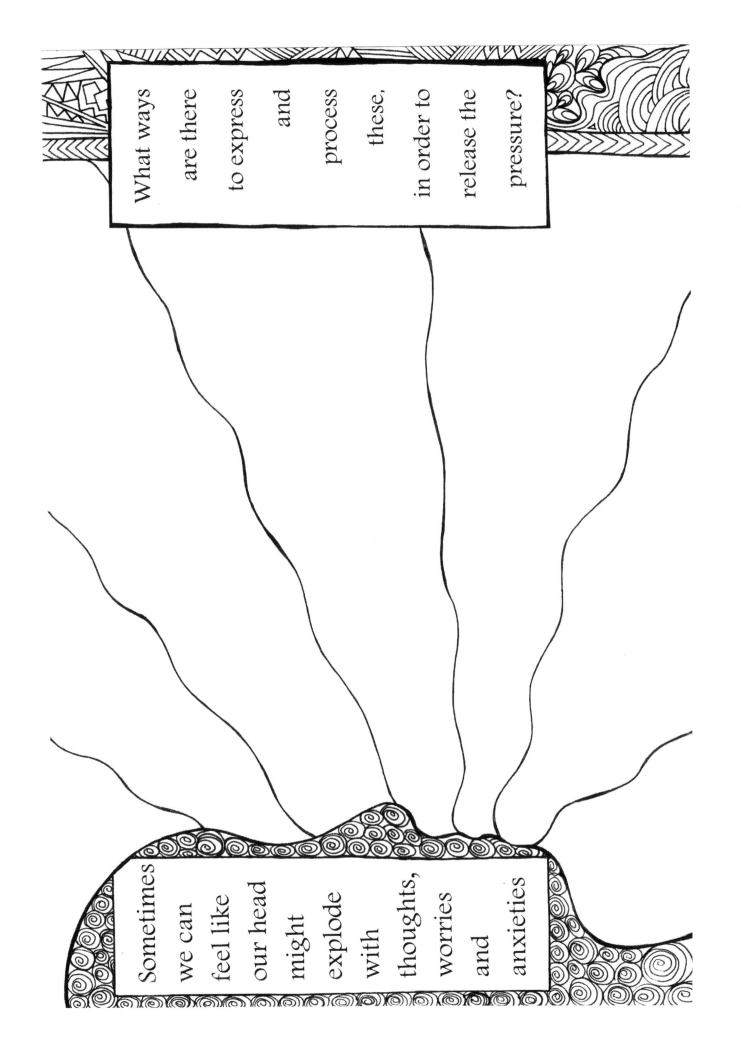

What ways are there to express and process these, in order to release the pressure?

Sometimes we can feel like our head might explode with thoughts, worries and anxieties

the sensations I notice in my body…

how I express it…

my associations with this emotion…

pick an

emotion

you

feel

a lot

These boats can carry heavy loads –
put your worries and fears inside them.
Visualize untying the ropes and watching
the wind carry them out to sea.

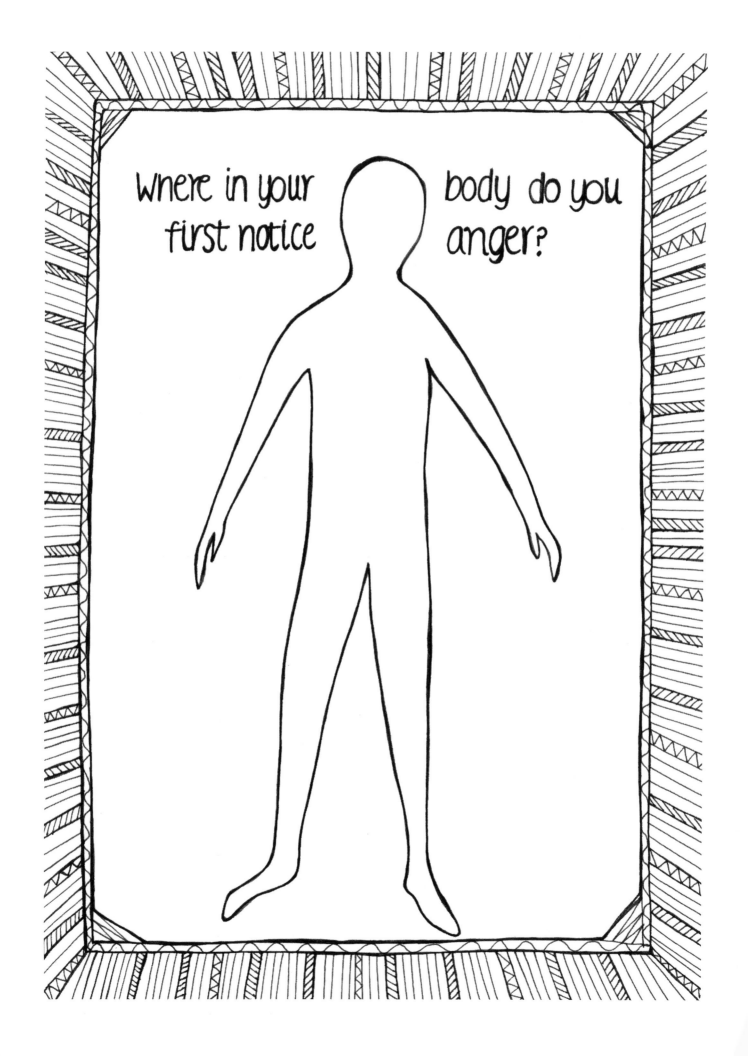

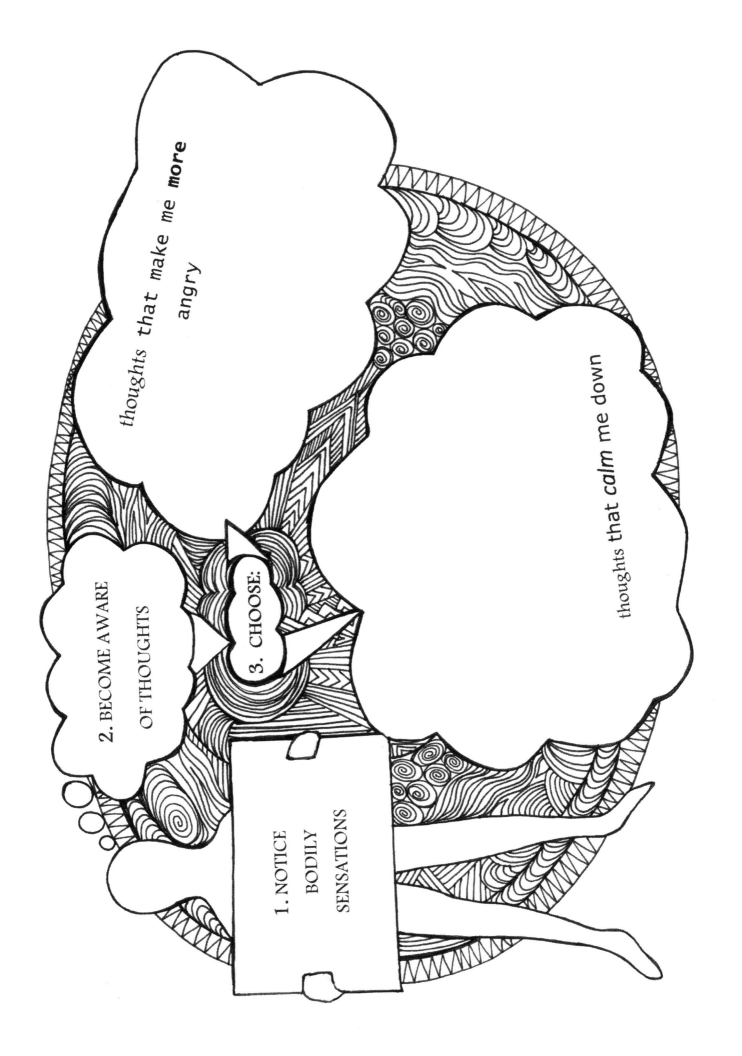

If your anxiety was a monster,

what would it look like?

What feeds it?

What starves and shrinks it?

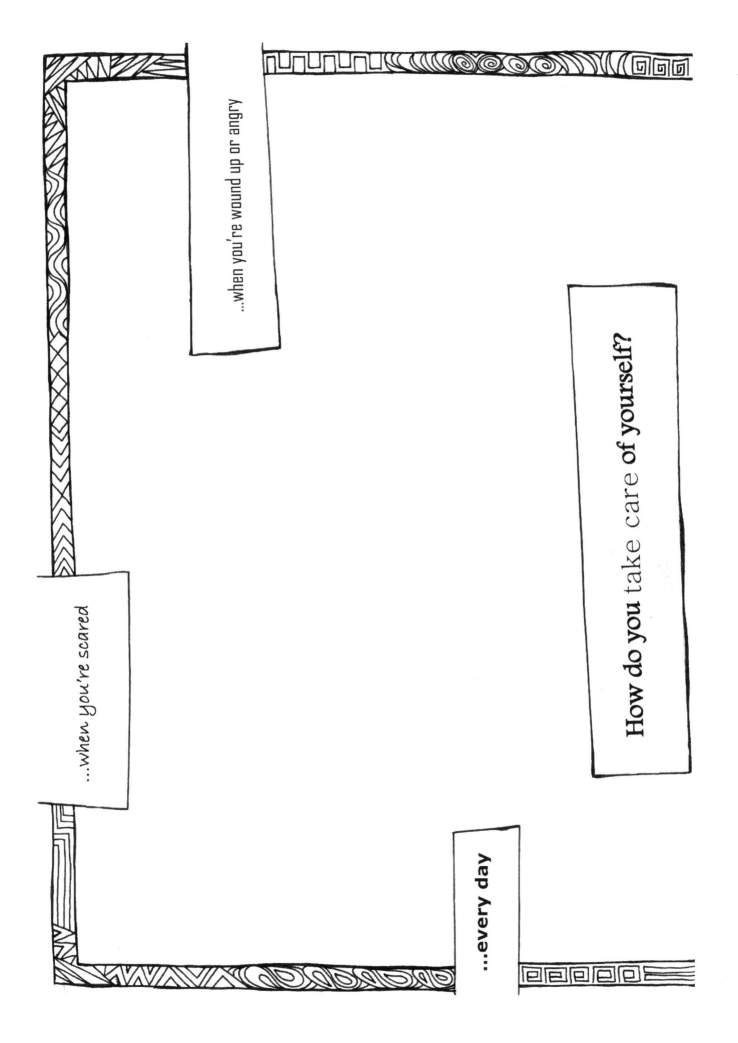

...when you're wound up or angry

How do you take care of yourself?

...when you're scared

...every day

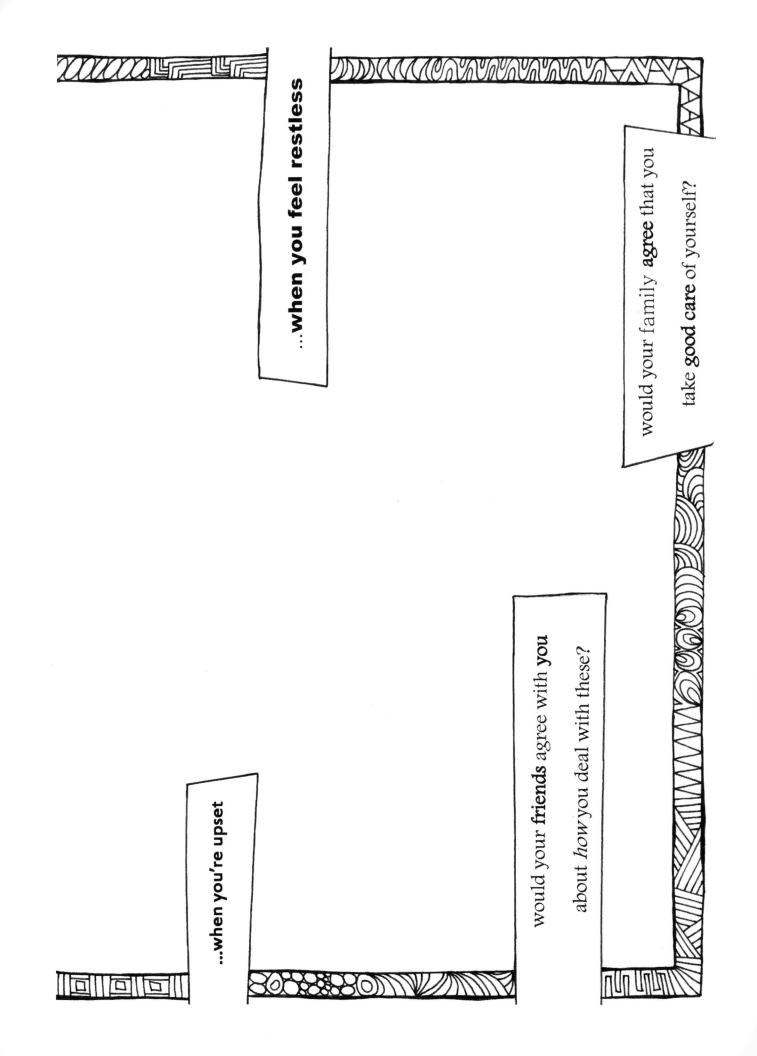

...when you feel restless

would your family **agree** that you take **good care** of yourself?

...when you're upset

would your **friends** agree with **you** about *how* you deal with these?

Ways to look after myself

physically:

mentally:

emotionally:

spiritually:

Ways to **raise** my mood

action

interpersonal

cognitive

what I liked about

before

What's better about

NOW

What I miss the most is...

and next...

and next...

Chapter 3

Reflecting, Problem Solving, Goal Setting

We all arrive at solutions to our problems in a variety of ways. Some people rely heavily on their instincts to inform decision-making, others prefer to analyse and let their logic prevail, whilst some use a combination of both. There is also a wide range in the amount of time we spend on solving problems. For example, adolescents are more likely to be spontaneous and impulsive than those who obsess and endlessly ruminate over worries.

The worksheets in this chapter are aimed at clients focusing on establishing and understanding their individualistic ways of dealing with problem solving. The first worksheets help clients reflect on their past, including how effective previous decision-making strategies have been. It can be useful to gain an understanding about these, before exploring what the future could look like. This can involve helping clients identify what steps and changes are needed for them to implement, in order for them to achieve their goals.

Exploration through artistic means can inspire us to think more creatively, leading to new, insightful ideas. This stimulates the right hemisphere of our brains, as discovered by Betty Edwards. In *The New Drawing on the Right Side of the Brain*, she writes about how the stimulation of drawing can provide new perceptions and a whole different approach to problem solving. She states: 'Creative solutions to problems, whether personal or professional, will be accessible through new modes of thinking and new ways of using the power of your whole brain' (Edwards 2008, p.6).

Identifying goals

Realistic and achievable goal setting can be adversely affected by low self-esteem and core beliefs about our abilities. Failure can be hard to take if our confidence is low, and so we're more likely to set lower goals which do not reflect our capabilities. Conversely, someone else may set overly high goals so that the failure in achieving them proves to the person that their core belief is right, that they are not 'good enough' or that they are a failure.

Often the obstacles to us achieving our dreams are ourselves and the beliefs we hold. The latter worksheets in this chapter focus on identifying our goals, our ambitions and dreams, and what the obstacles in the way might be. Thinking about who and what inspires us is essential for motivation. It can also be helpful to break down these goals into smaller bite-sized chunks, so that a client doesn't feel overwhelmed by the enormity of where they want to be and give up without trying.

Emotional wellbeing can be enhanced enormously when we feel proud of ourselves and our achievements. Spending time in therapy to reflect on our previous choices and work out what we want for our future is vital for our journey towards fulfilment.

LIFE PATH SO FAR

Date

Include important people, events and experiences

choices I wouldn't
make again

decisions made by my head

decisions

made by my heart

If you had a magic wand, in what

order would you change things?

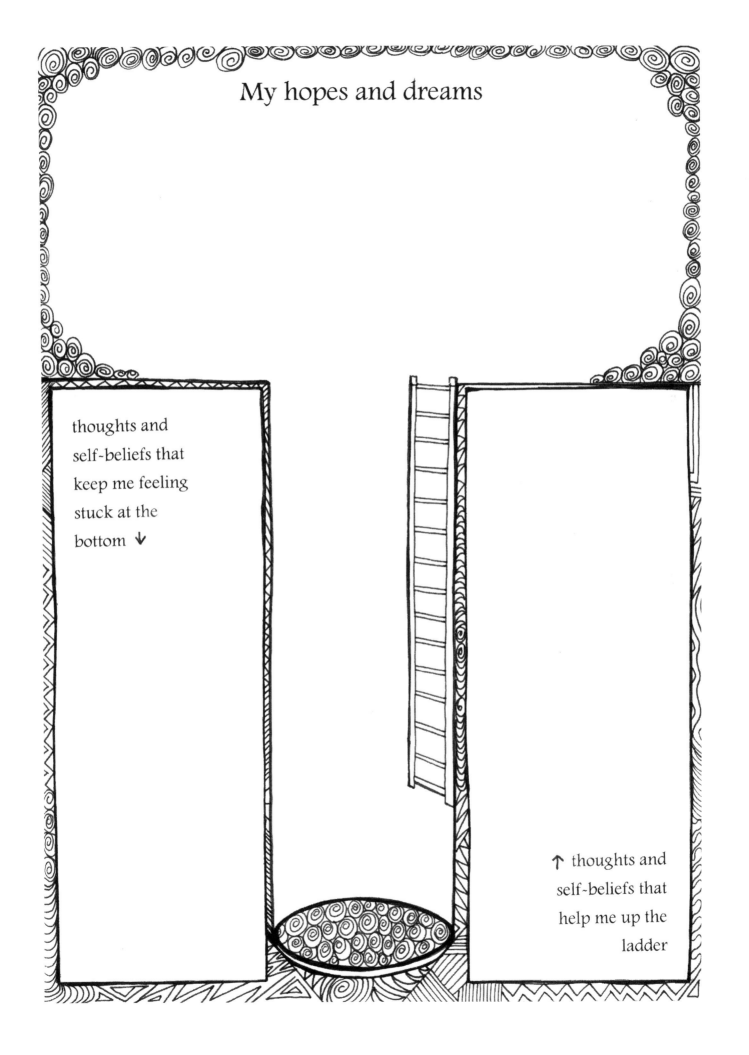

i dream of being...

who or what

INSPIRES me

how I get there...

where I want to be...

what could help me get there...

any blocks in the way...

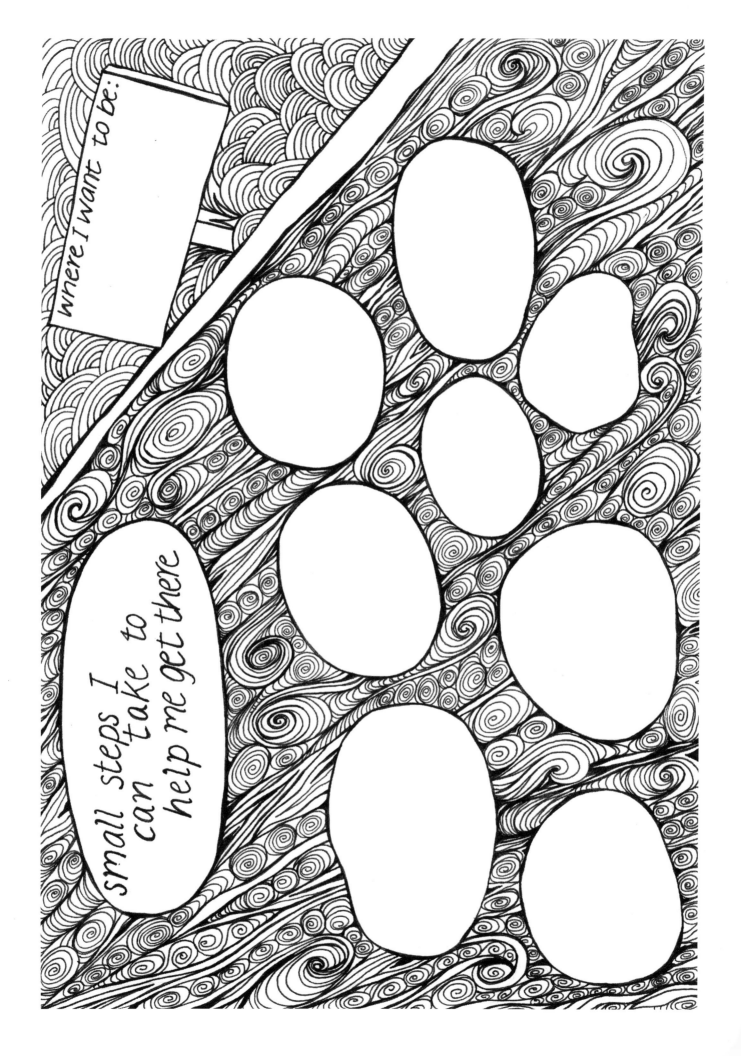

Part Two – Colouring Collection

Stress Management

Effective management of stress is vital for our wellbeing. It requires us to have a good level of understanding about ourselves, as different people are affected by different events and experiences. It is helpful to know these specifics and how we then react to and cope with stress.

Taking time out for relaxation is essential, especially when coping with stress. Most people find doing what they love to do is extremely effective. This works because it can provide a mental break from worrying and can also help us to process our experiences. Creativity is a well-known way of relaxing, as stated by Cathy A. Malchiodi. She explains how making art can:

> alleviate emotional stress and anxiety by creating a physiological response of relaxation or by altering mood…it is known that creative activity can actually increase brain levels of serotonin, the chemical linked to depression. Other people experience art as a form of meditation, finding inner peace and calm through art expression. (2007, p.14)

Chapter 4

The Alphabet

Creative activities are renowned for alleviating stress and this can be enhanced by working with colour and pattern. I've loved drawing these letters for clients to enjoy colouring in. The letters can be used solely for colouring in or be cut out and put together for making words and names or initials. I have found it's a lovely extension of sense of self and esteem-building work (especially for young people) to be given a collection of the letters spelling out their name.

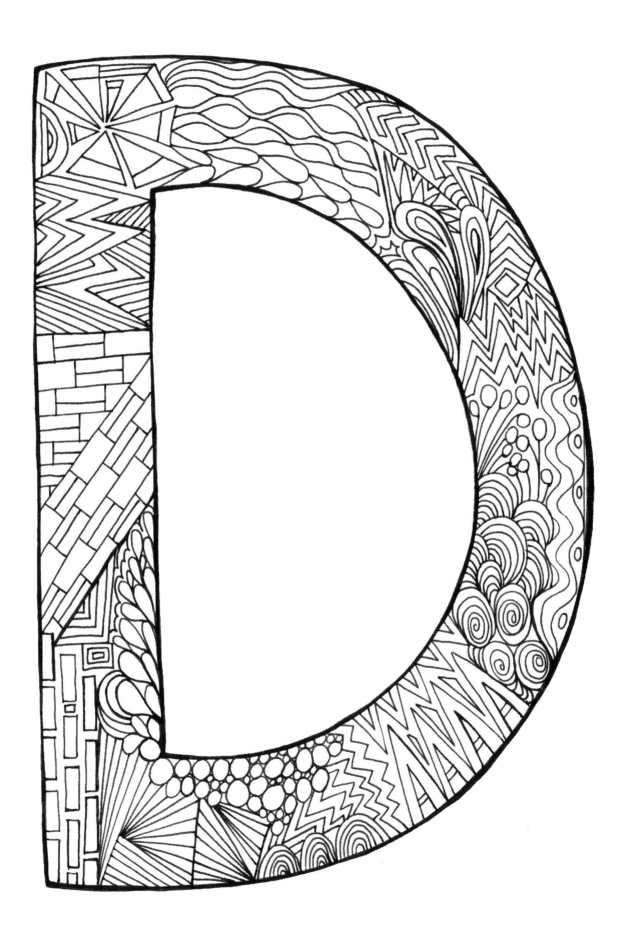

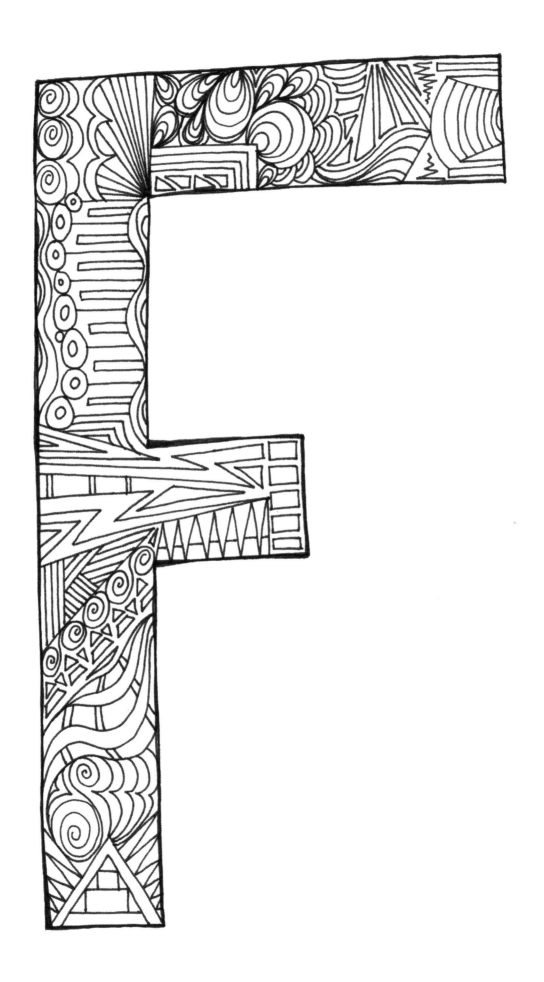

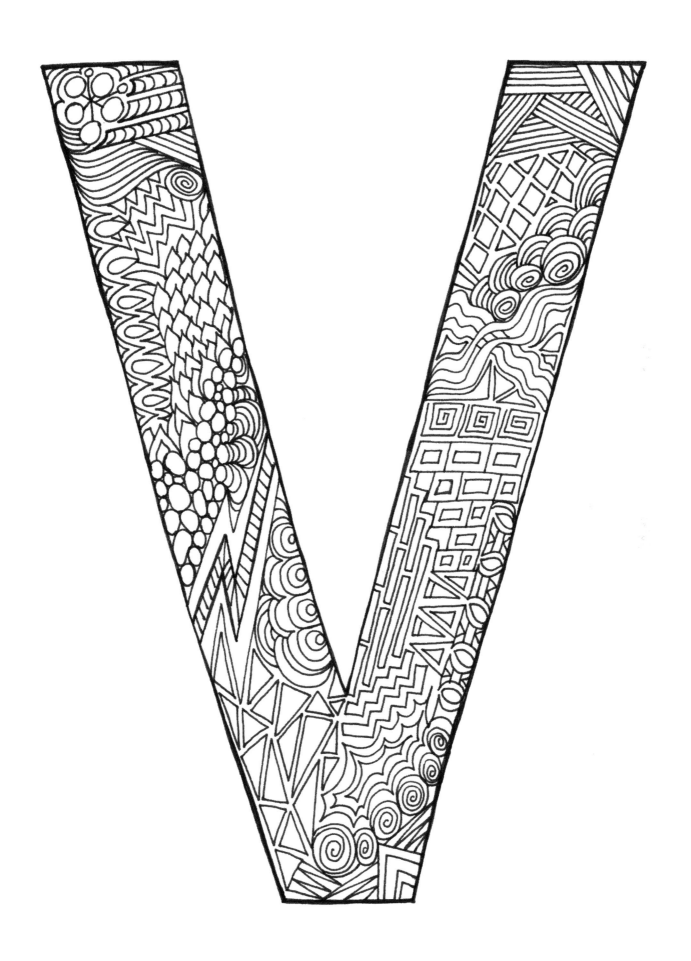

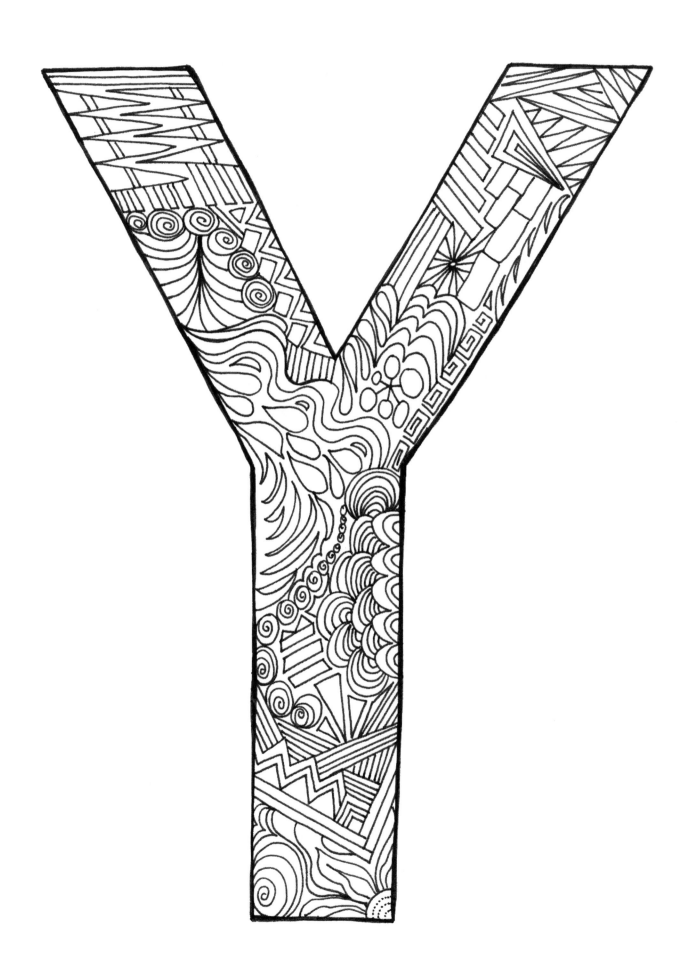

Chapter 5

Mandalas

The inspiration for the designs in this chapter came from the symbolic nature of mandalas, a word loosely translated from ancient Sanskrit to mean circle. Mandalas are spiritual and ritualistic symbols in Hinduism and Buddhism, representing the universe and all aspects of life and existence. Native Americans use them in healing rituals and they also can be used as tools for meditation.

Carl Jung used mandalas for personal growth, as well as for therapeutic purposes with clients. He saw mandalas as representational of our complexities and inner worlds, and believed that in the creating of mandalas a shift could be made, bringing things from the unconscious mind into consciousness. In his book *Mandala Symbolism* he states: 'Most mandalas have an intuitive, irrational character and, through their symbolic content, exert a retroactive influence on the unconscious' (Jung 1972, p.77). He believed that this symbolism could extend to encapsulate our entirety as an individual.

Others claim that the circular nature of mandalas connects us to the world and those around us. Lori Bailey Cunningham is the author of the beautiful book *The Mandala Book: Patterns of the Universe*. She writes: 'To become aware of the mandala is to become conscious of what is going on around us, and it is this consciousness that helps us see our connection to the world and one another' (Cunningham 2010, p.2).

There are many books available charting the use of mandalas throughout history, as well as those teaching the practical aspects of creating your own, such as *Creating Mandalas: For Insight, Healing, and Self-Expression* by Susanne F. Fincher (2010). Others, such as *Mandala Workbook for Inner Self Discovery* by Anneke Huyser (2002), focus on healing and personal growth. There are also kits available, combining workbooks with meditations. For further artistic inspiration there is a book packed with contemporary mandalas and design techniques called *Zen Mandalas: Sacred Circles Inspired by Zentangle* by Suzanne McNeill (2011).

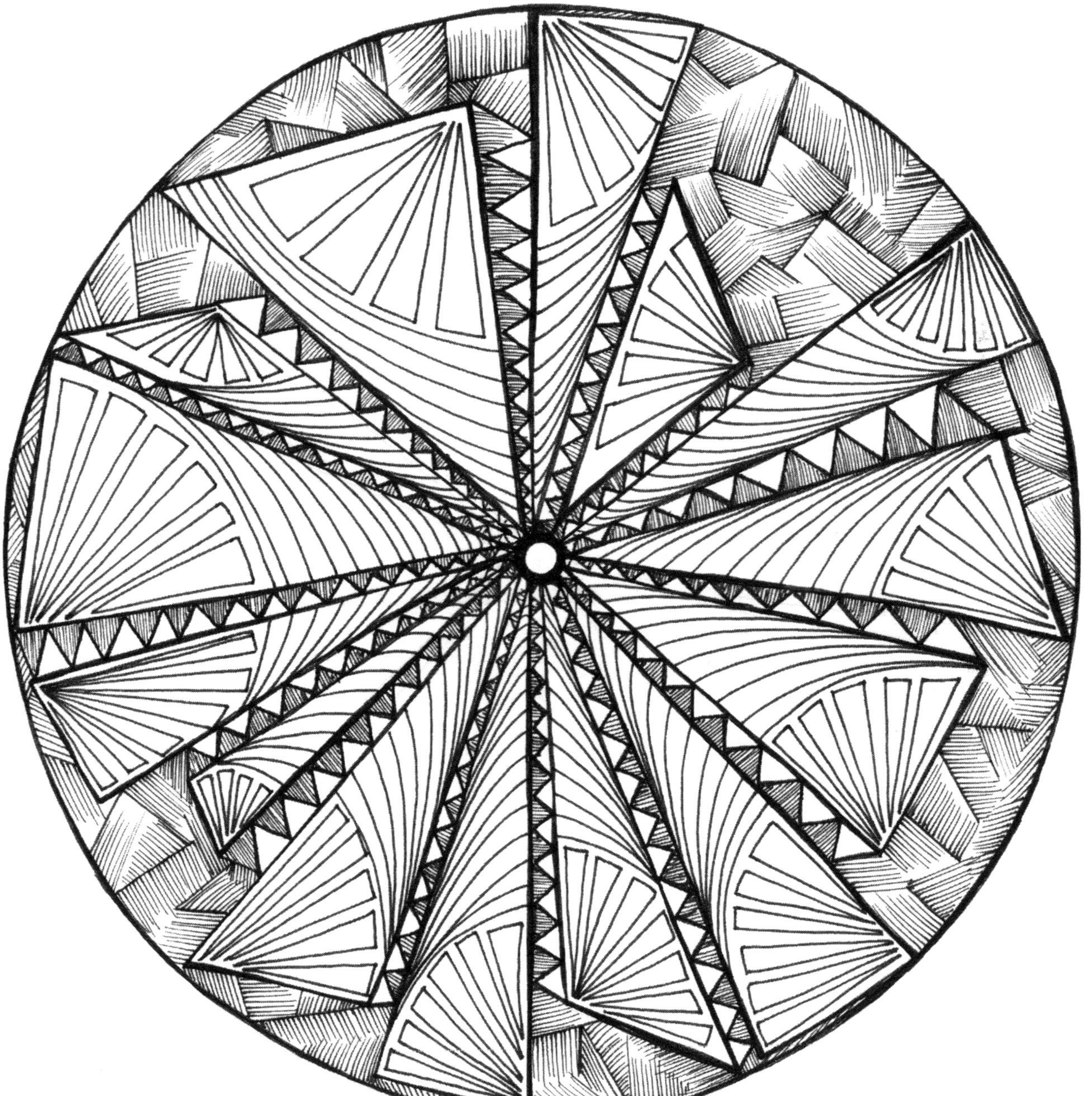

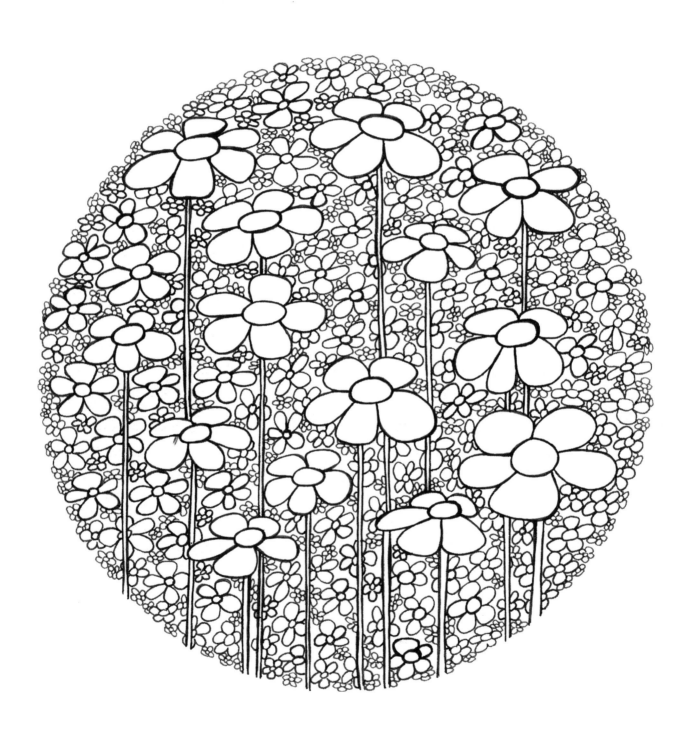

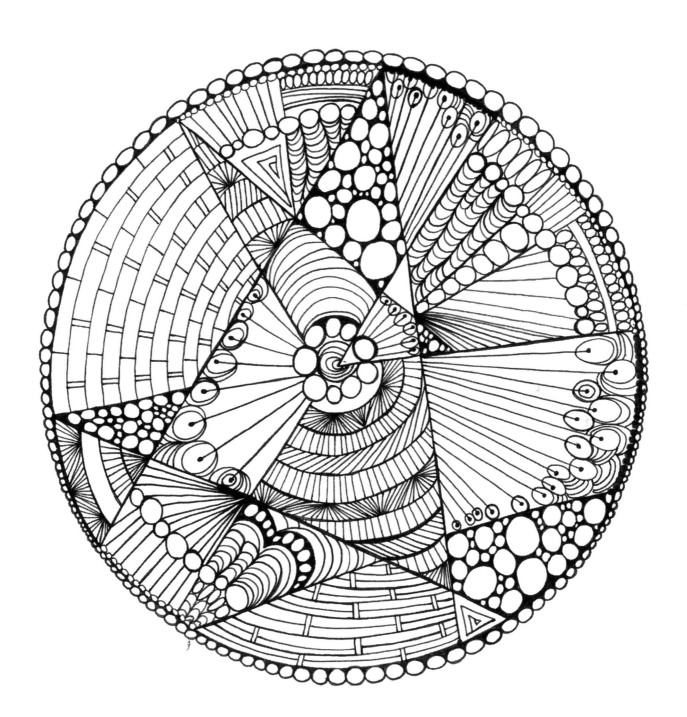

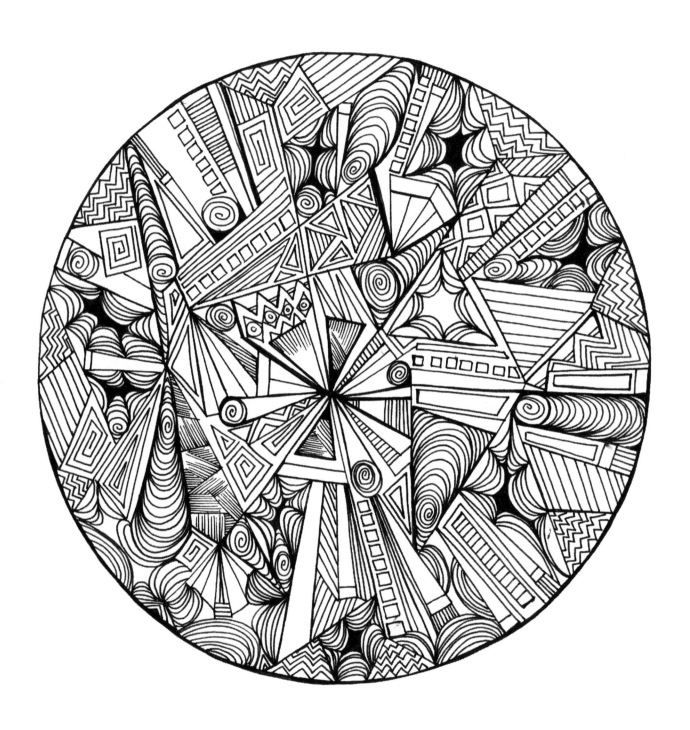

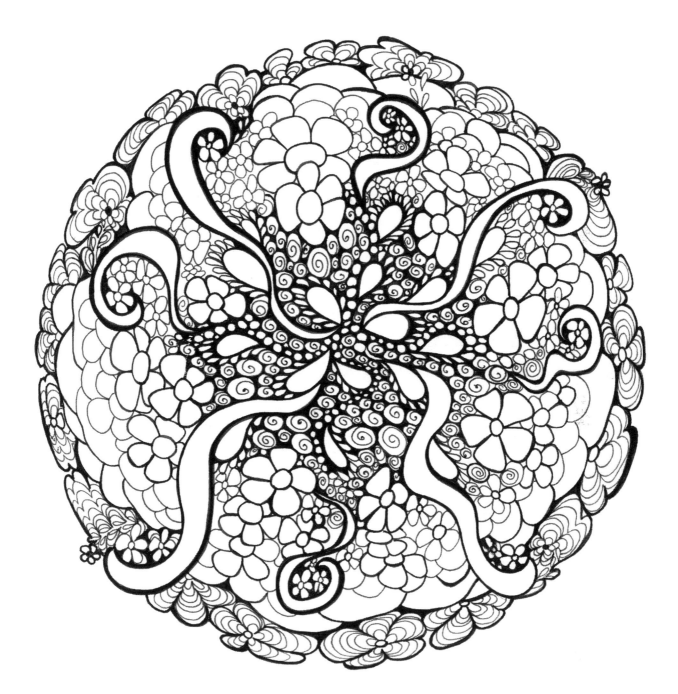

References

Beck, J. S. (1995) *Cognitive Therapy: Basics and Beyond.* New York, NY: Guilford Press.

Cunningham, L. B. (2010) *The Mandala Book: Patterns of the Universe.* New York, NY: Sterling Publishing.

Edwards, B. (2008) *The New Drawing on the Right Side of the Brain.* (First published 1979) London: Harper Collins.

Ellis, A. and Drydan, W. (1997) *The Practice of Rational Emotive Behaviour Therapy.* New York, NY: Springer.

Fincher, S. F. (2010) *Creating Mandalas: For Insight, Healing, and Self-Expression.* Boston, MA: Shambhala Publications.

Huyser, A. (2002) *Mandala Workbook for Inner Self Discovery.* Havelte: Binkey Kok.

Jung, C. G. (1972) *Mandala Symbolism.* Princeton, NJ: Princeton University Press.

Malchiodi, C. A. (2007) *The Art Therapy Sourcebook.* New York, NY: McGraw-Hill.

McNeill, S. (2011) *Zen Mandalas: Sacred Circles Inspired by Zentangle.* East Petersburg, PA: Fox Chapel Publishing.

Neenan, M. and Drydan, W. (2004) *Cognitive Therapy: 100 Key Points & Techniques.* Hove: Brunner-Routledge.

Plummer, D. (2010) *Helping Adolescents and Adults to Build Self-Esteem.* London: Jessica Kingsley Publishers.

Roberts, R. and Thomas, M. (2012) *The Book of Zentangle.* Whitinsville, MA: Zentangle Inc.

Stevens, R. (1996) *Understanding the Self.* London: Sage Publications.